A

MW01688637

Book of 30 Postcards

TODTRI

This book was designed and produced by BSB Publishing bv
Printed and bound in Belgium

ISBN 1-57717-143-8

This edition published in the U.S. by
TODTRI Book Publishers
P.O. Box 572, New York, NY 10116-0572
Fax: (212) 695-6984
e-mail: info@todtri.com

Visit us on the web!
www.todtri.com

AUGUSTE RENOIR
1841-1919

Pierre-Auguste Renoir, one of the famous masters of impressionism, began his career as a decorative painter for plates and teapots at the Sèvres porcelain factory. Left penniless as a consequence of the progressive color printing process, he decided to train himself to become an artist. It was in the studio of the Swiss master Gleyre - a friendly man who asked for little money from his students, but as part of their art education allowed them to perform plays - where he became acquainted with Monet, Bazille and Sisley. Together with them he went out into the wilderness and frequented the Café Guerbois on the Avenue de Clichy, where Manet, Pisarro, Degas and Cézanne were to be found regularly. It was the core of the group which, in 1874, established the 'Société anonyme des Artistes Peintres, Sculpteurs, Graveurs', so that, independent from the academic painters who laid down the law and in spite of all condemnation, they could organize their own exhibitions.

Whilst other impressionists such as Monet, Sisley and Cézanne sought inspiration from nature and the landscape, Renoir was an outstanding example of a figure painter. He was also a master in conveying atmosphere, the tricks of the sunlight through foliage, which he demonstrated, for example, with great compositions like *Moulin de la Galette or Déjeuner des Canotiers (The Boatmen's Lunch)*, but his main aim - no less revolutionary at that time - was the portrayal of ordinary people in their daily surroundings.

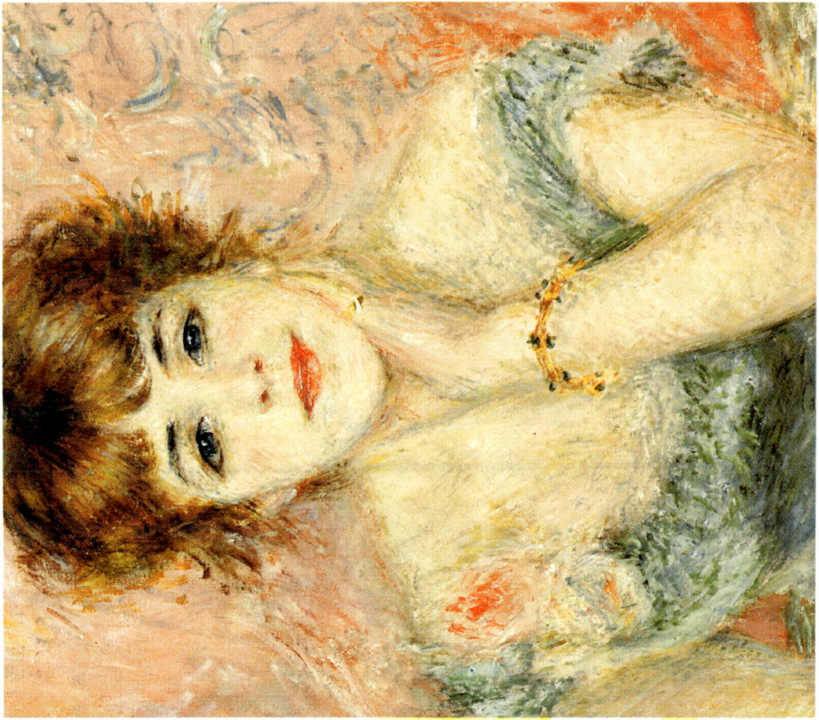

Auguste Renoir, *Portrait of Jeanne Samary*, 1877.
Pushkin Museum of Fine Arts, Moscow.

Auguste Renoir Book of 30 Postcards - BSB Publishing - The Hague - Holland

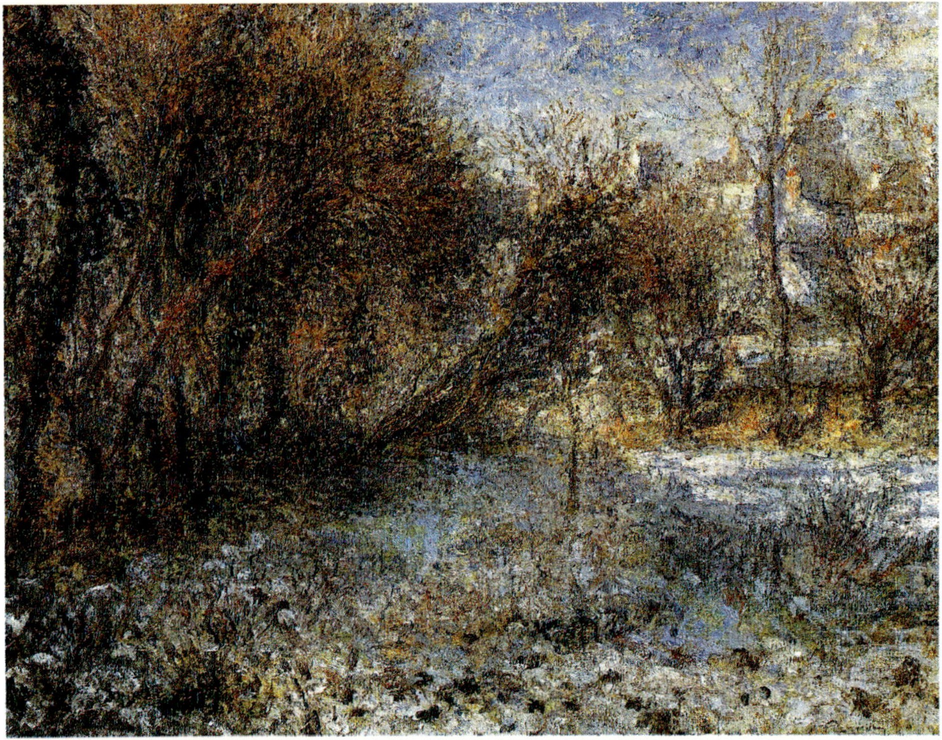

Auguste Renoir, *Landscape with Snow*, c. 1875.
Musée de l'Orangerie, Paris.

Auguste Renoir Book of 30 Postcards - BSB Publishing - The Hague - Holland

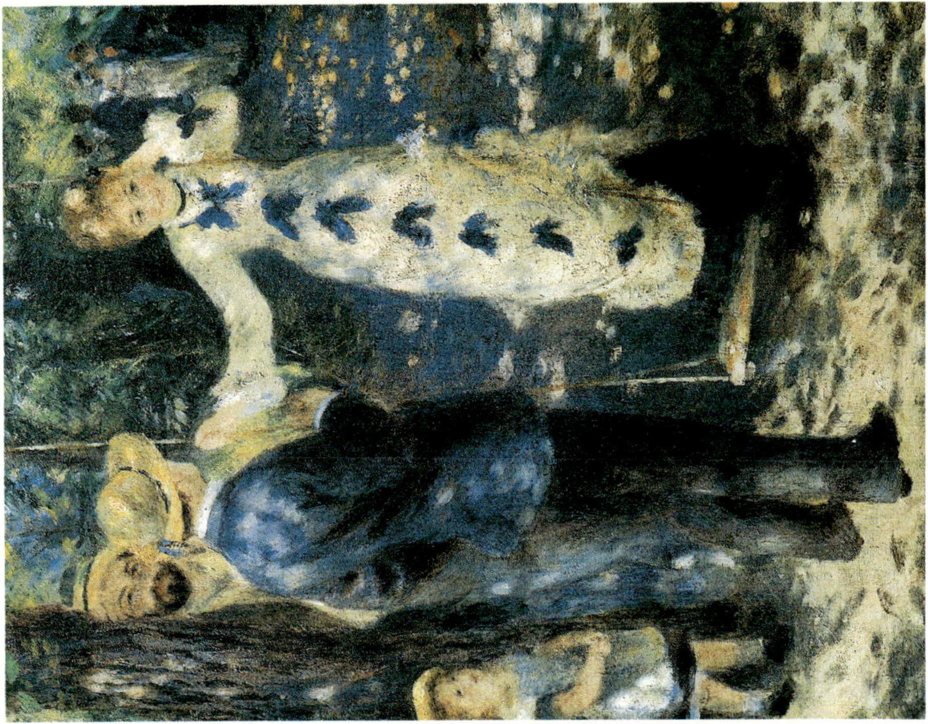

Auguste Renoir, *The Swing,* 1876.
Musée d'Orsay, Paris.

Auguste Renoir Book of 30 Postcards - BSB Publishing - The Hague - Holland

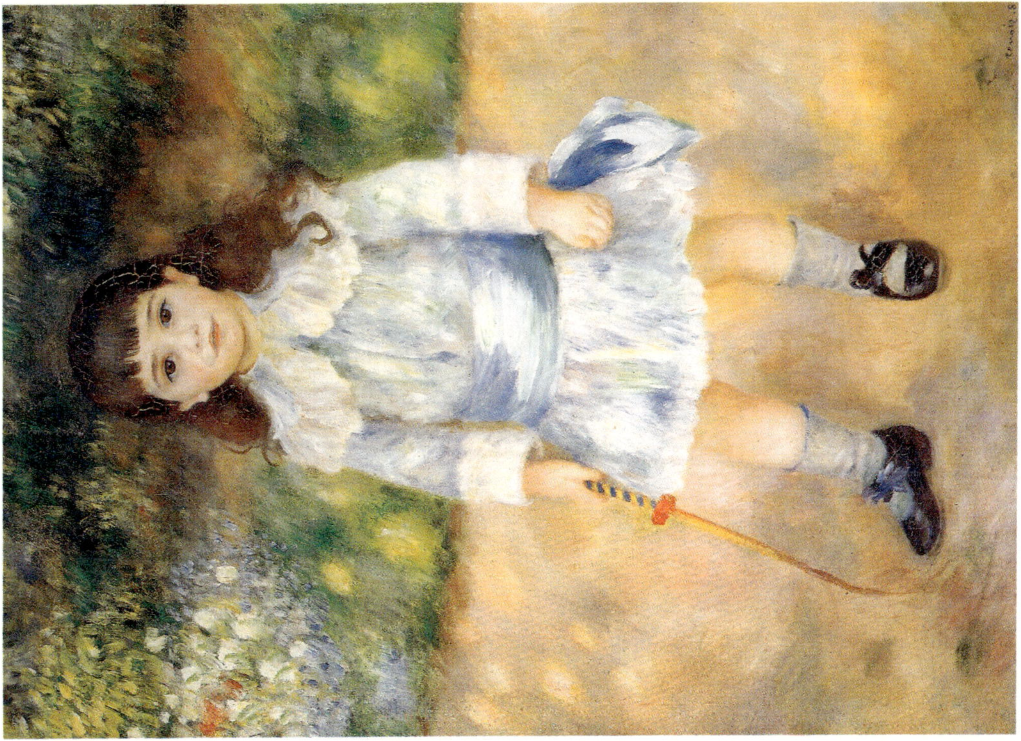

Auguste Renoir, *Child with a Whip*, 1885.
Hermitage, St. Petersburg.

Auguste Renoir Book of 30 Postcards - BSB Publishing - The Hague - Holland

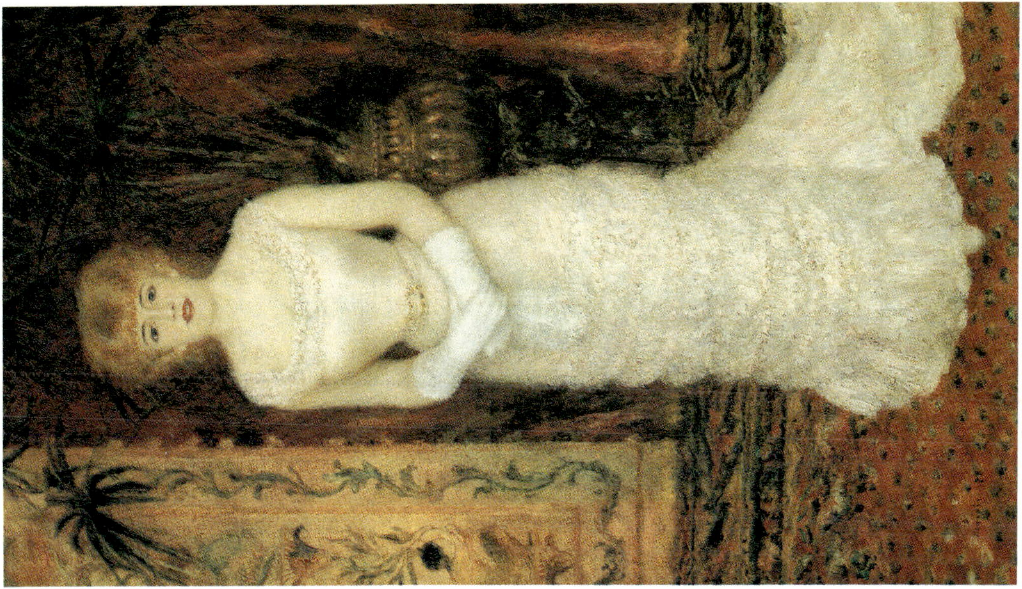

Auguste Renoir, *Jeanne Samary*, 1878.
Hermitage, St. Petersburg.

Auguste Renoir Book of 30 Postcards - BSB Publishing - The Hague - Holland

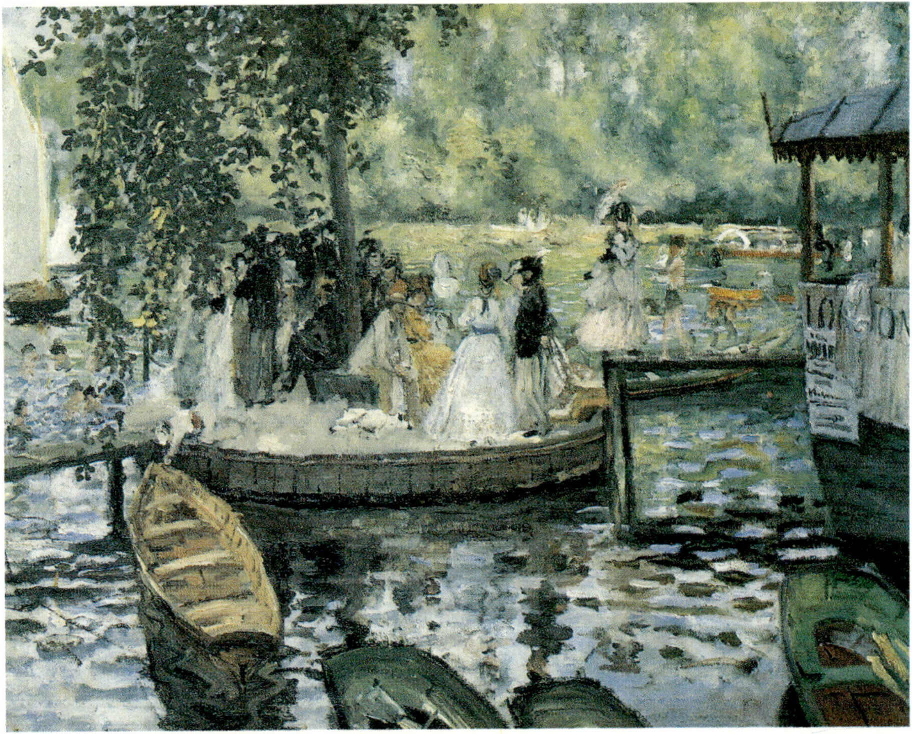

Auguste Renoir, *La Grenouillère,* 1868-69.
Nationalmuseum, Stockholm.

Auguste Renoir Book of 30 Postcards - BSB Publishing - The Hague - Holland

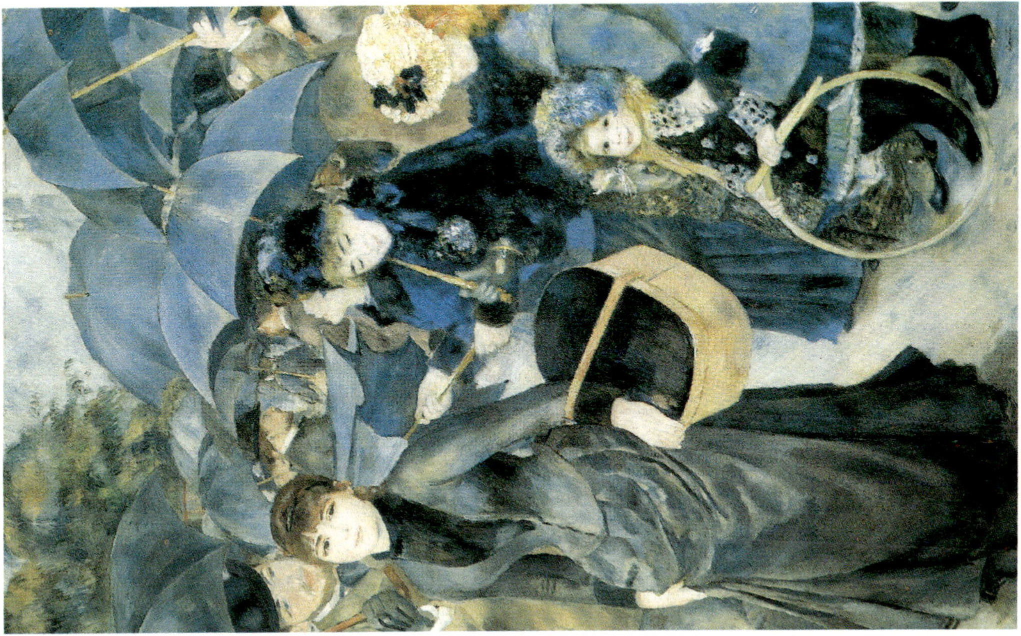

Auguste Renoir, *The Umbrellas*, 1883.
National Gallery, London.

Auguste Renoir Book of 30 Postcards - BSB Publishing - The Hague - Holland

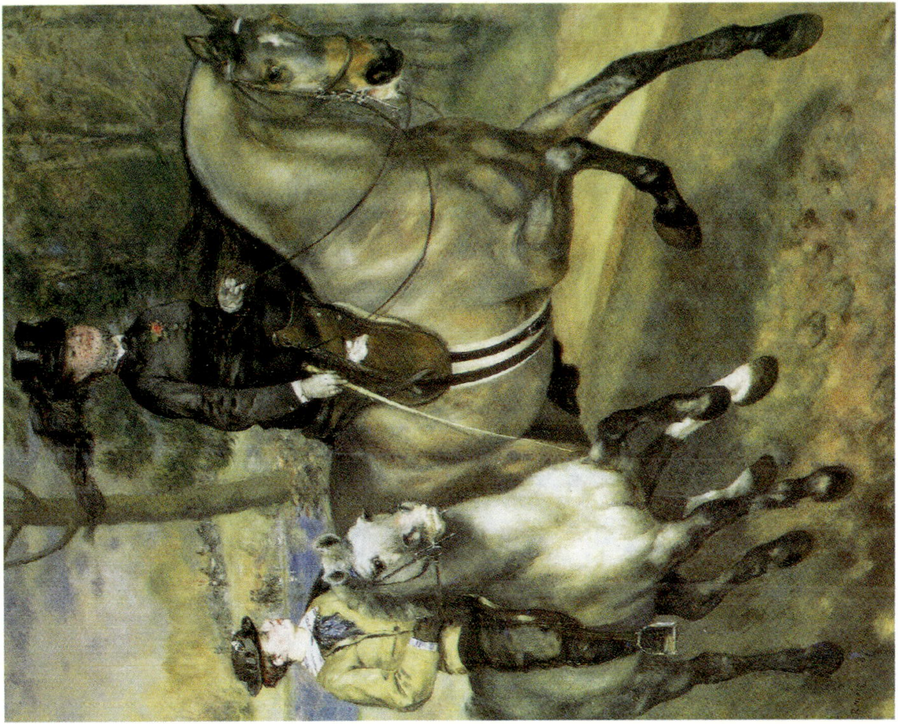

Auguste Renoir, *Riders in the Bois de Boulogne*, 1873.
Kunsthalle, Hamburg.

Auguste Renoir Book of 30 Postcards - BSB Publishing - The Hague - Holland

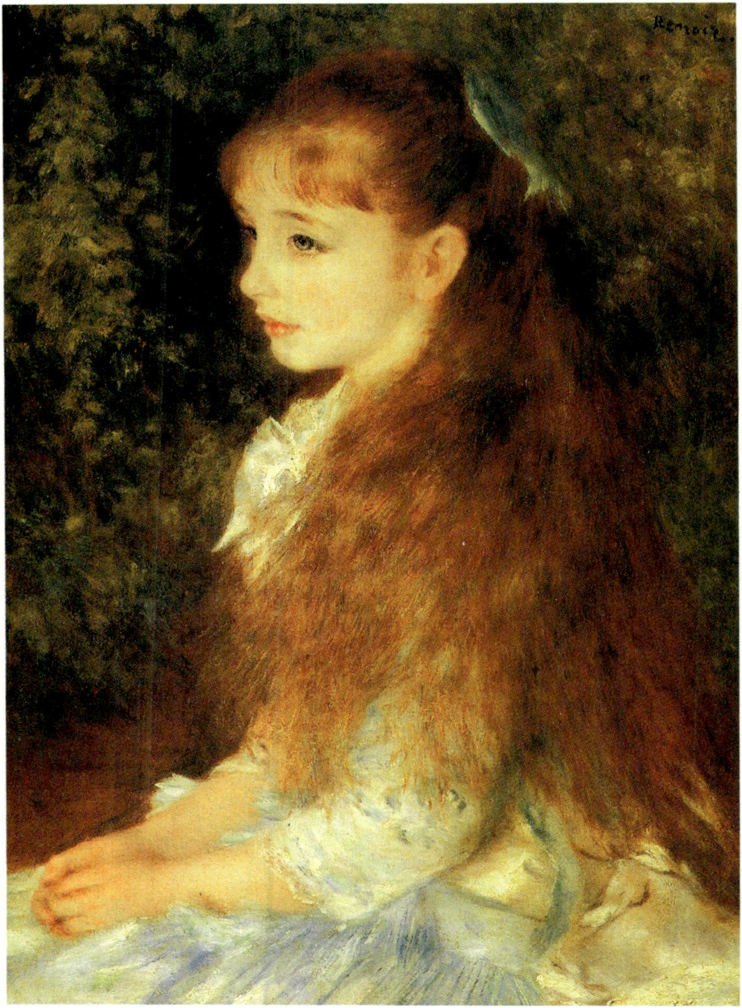
Renoir

Auguste Renoir, *Irène Cahen d'Anvers*, 1880.
Bührle Collection, Zurich.

Auguste Renoir Book of 30 Postcards - BSB Publishing - The Hague - Holland

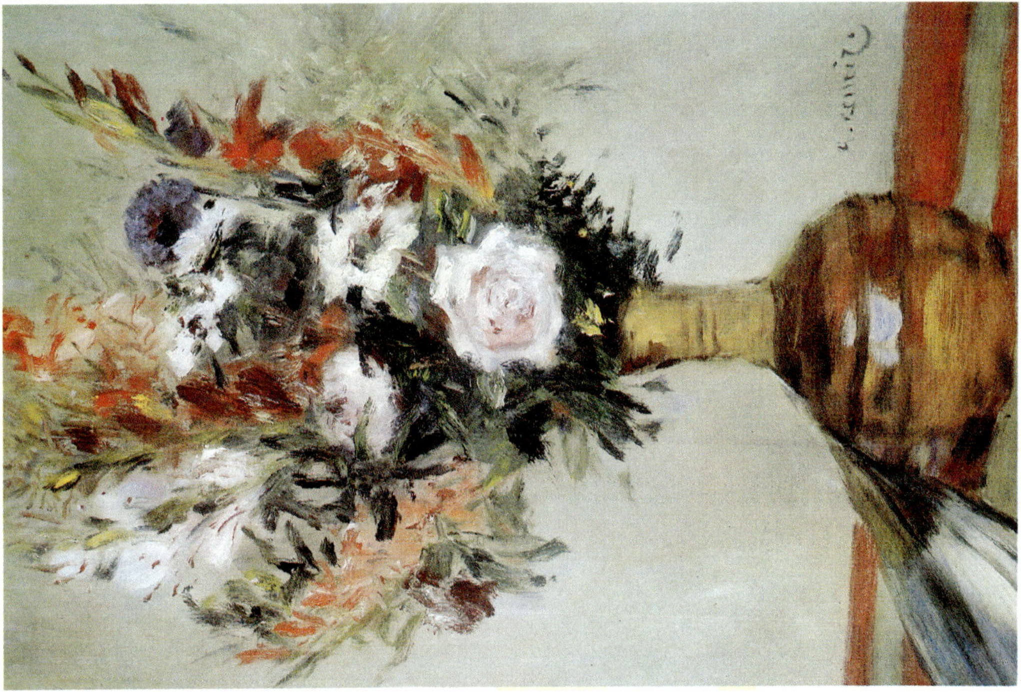

Auguste Renoir, *Flowers in a Vase*, c. 1872.
Private collection.

Auguste Renoir Book of 30 Postcards - BSB Publishing - The Hague - Holland

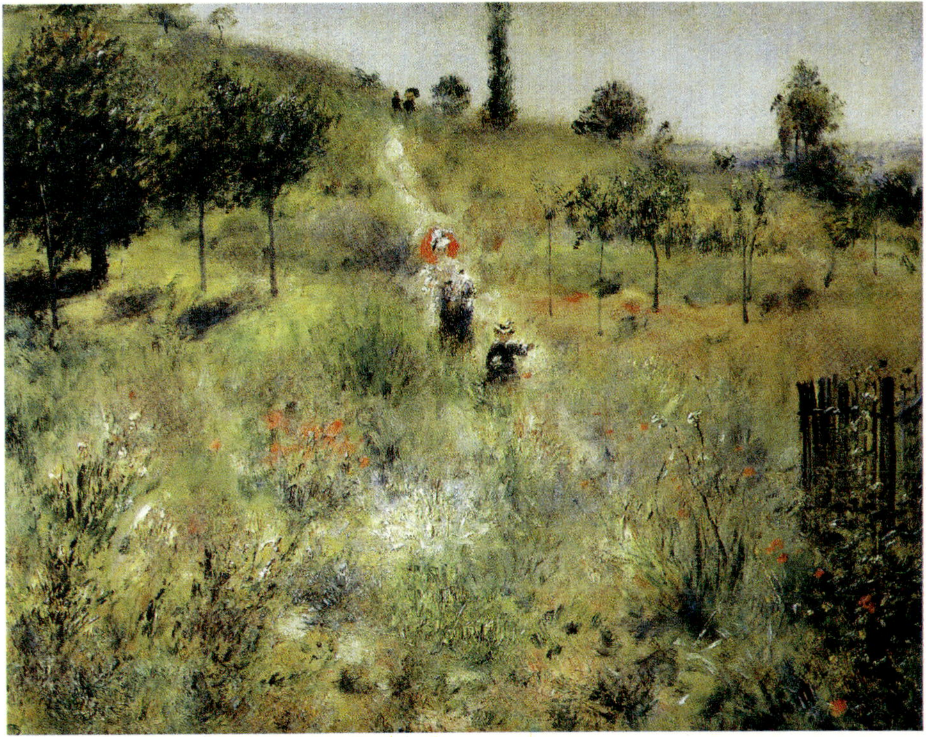

Auguste Renoir, *Path through Long Grass*, 1874.
Musée d'Orsay, Paris.

Auguste Renoir Book of 30 Postcards - BSB Publishing - The Hague - Holland

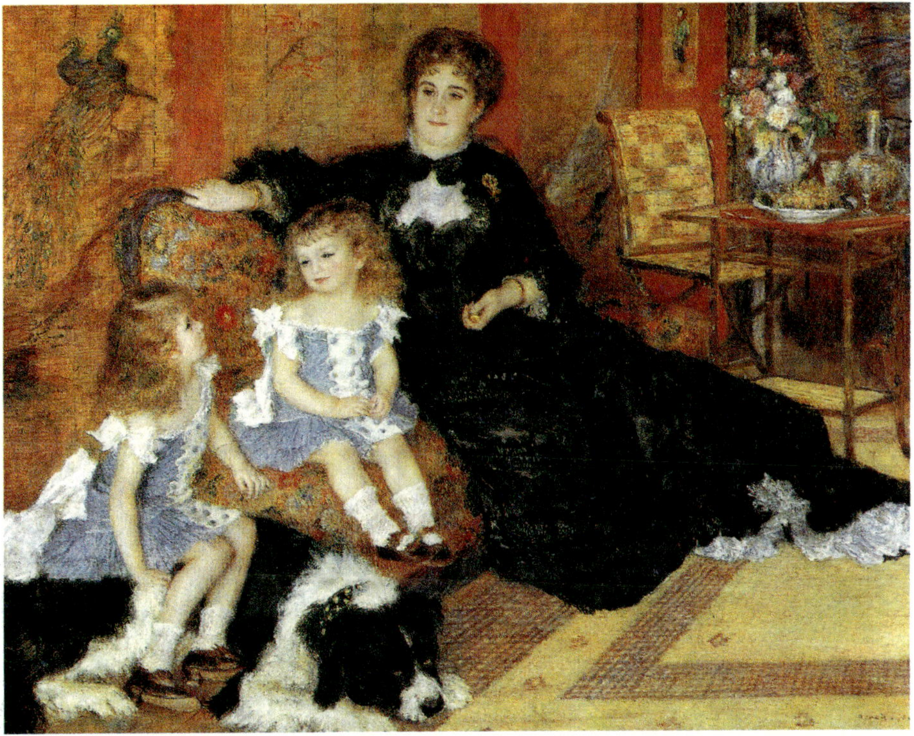

Auguste Renoir, *Madame Charpentier and her Children*, 1878.
Metropolitan Museum of Art, New York.

Auguste Renoir Book of 30 Postcards - BSB Publishing - The Hague - Holland

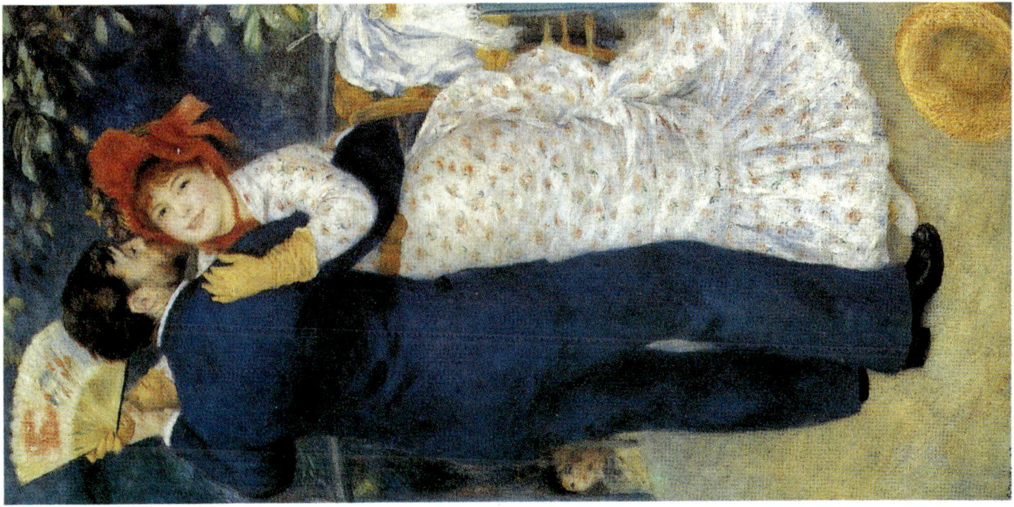

Auguste Renoir, *Dance in the Country*, 1882-83.
Musée d'Orsay, Paris.

Auguste Renoir Book of 30 Postcards - BSB Publishing - The Hague - Holland

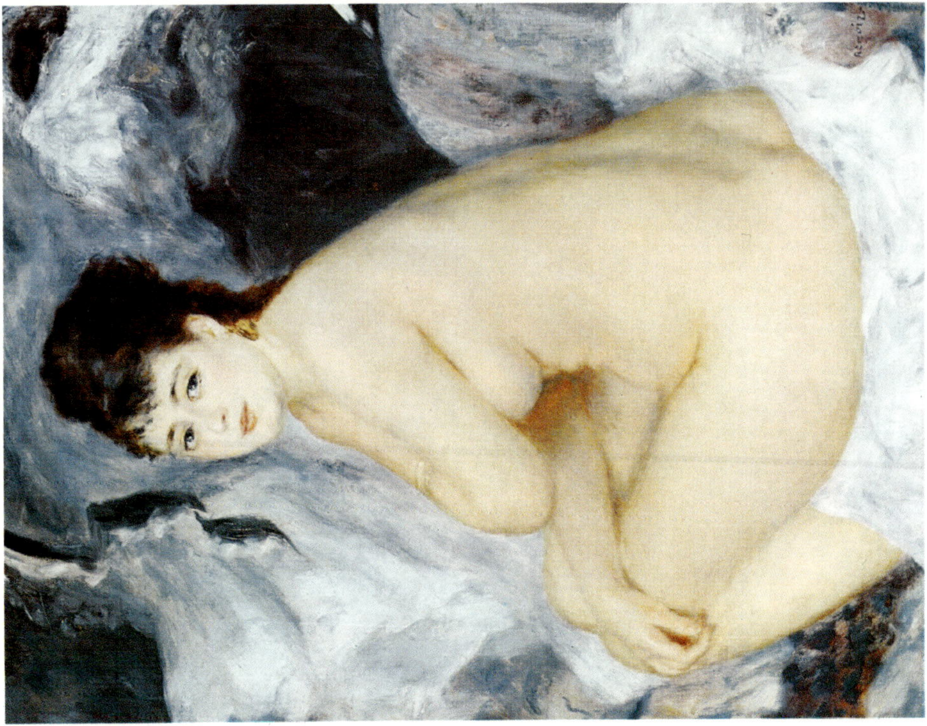

Auguste Renoir, *Nude on the sofa*, 1876.
Pushkin Museum of Fine Arts, Moscow.

Auguste Renoir Book of 30 Postcards - BSB Publishing - The Hague - Holland

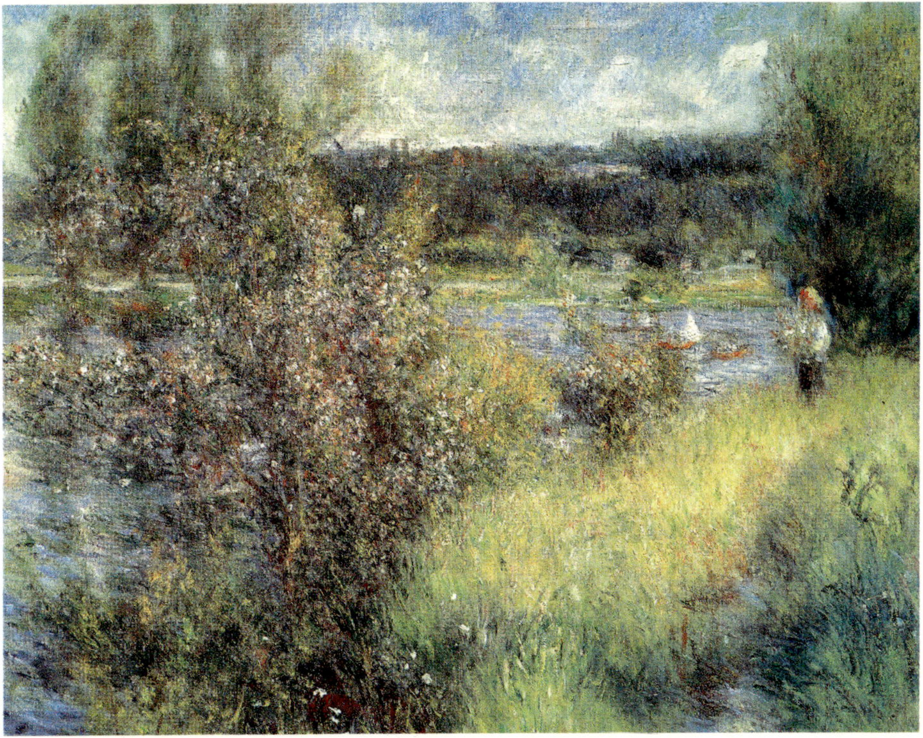

Auguste Renoir, *The Seine at Chatou,* 1880.
Museum of Fine Arts, Boston.

Auguste Renoir Book of 30 Postcards - BSB Publishing - The Hague - Holland

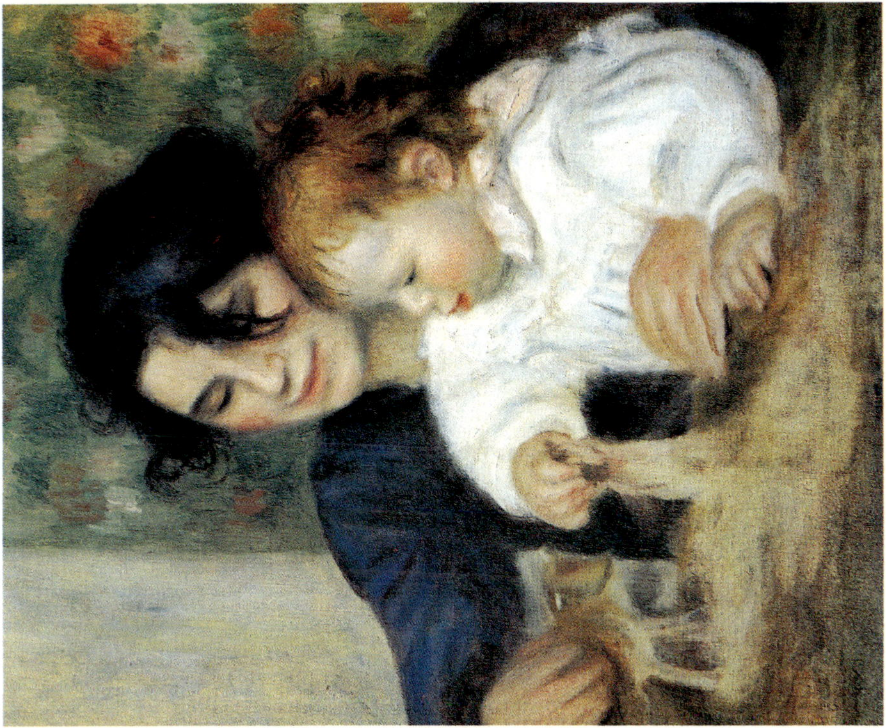

Auguste Renoir, *Gabrielle and Jean,* 1895.
Musée de l'Orangerie, Paris.

Auguste Renoir Book of 30 Postcards - BSB Publishing - The Hague - Holland

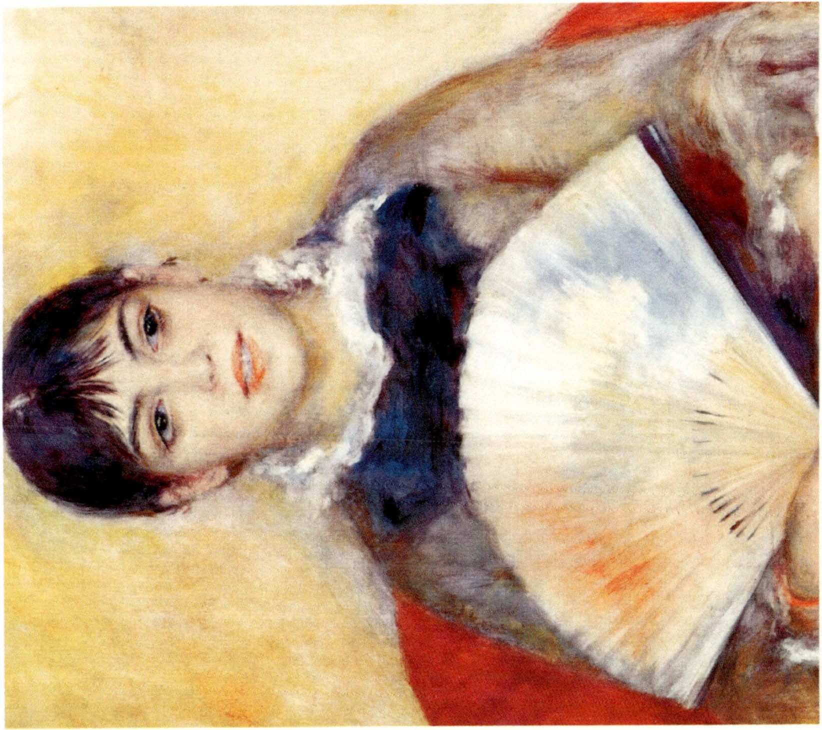

Auguste Renoir, *Young Woman with a Fan*, 1880.
Hermitage, St. Petersburg.

Auguste Renoir Book of 30 Postcards - BSB Publishing - The Hague - Holland

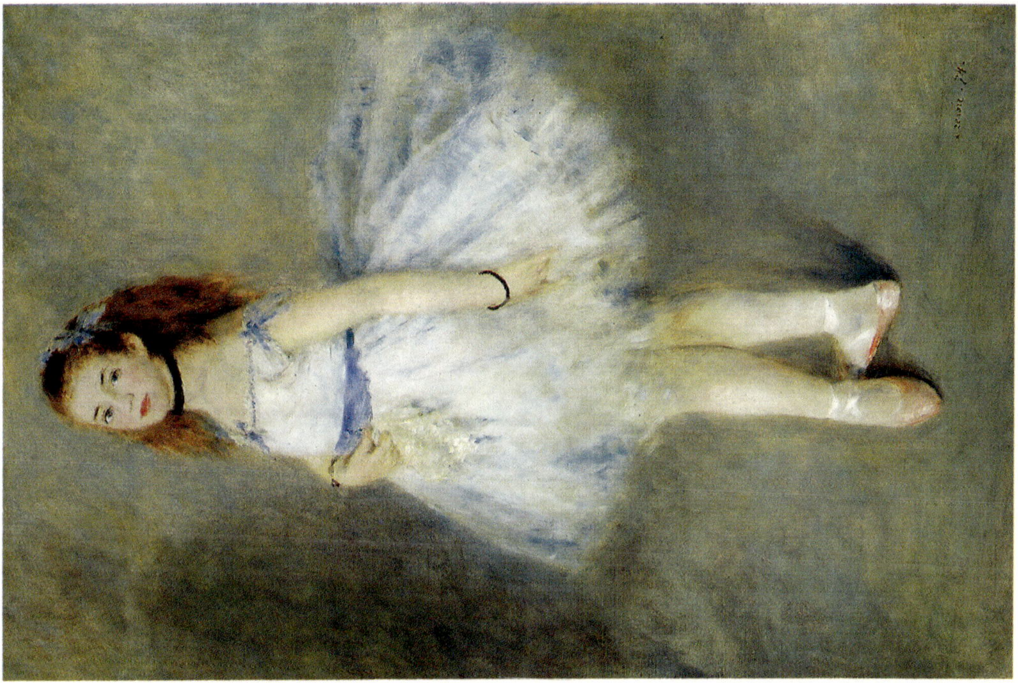

Auguste Renoir, *The Dancer,* 1874.
National Gallery of Art, Washington D.C.

Auguste Renoir Book of 30 Postcards - BSB Publishing - The Hague - Holland

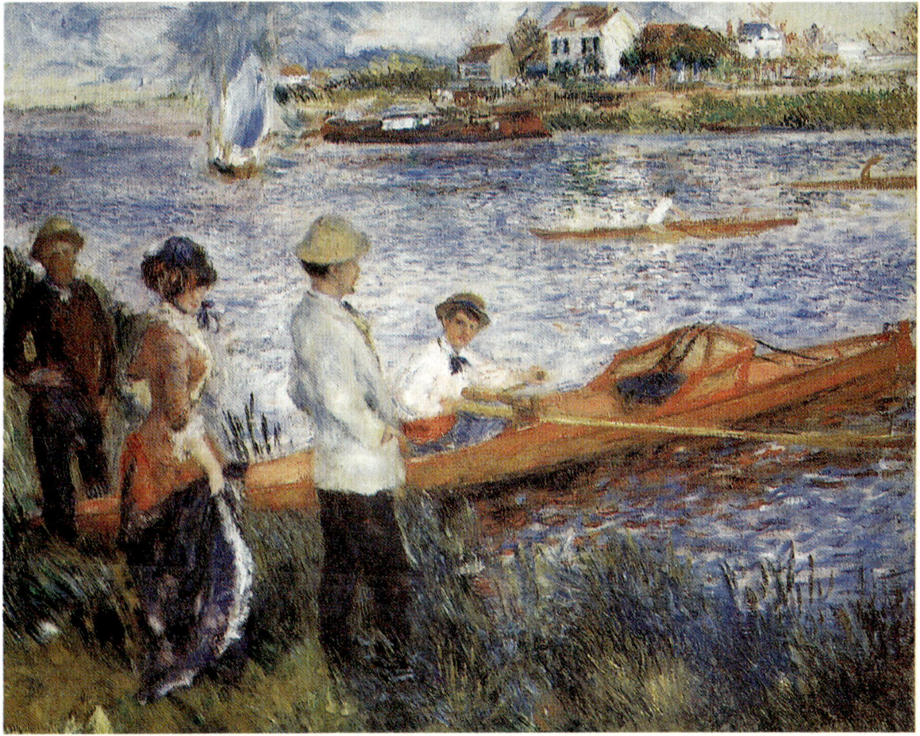

Auguste Renoir, *Oarsmen at Chatou*, 1879.
National Gallery of Art, Washington D.C.

Auguste Renoir Book of 30 Postcards - BSB Publishing - The Hague - Holland

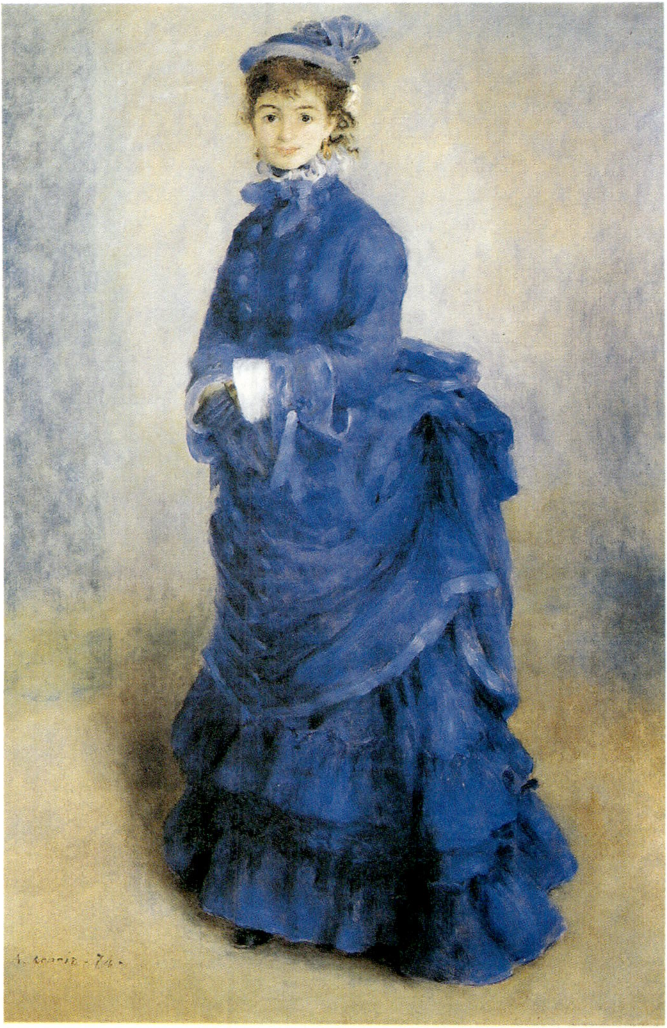

Auguste Renoir, *The Lady in Blue*, 1874.
National Museum of Wales, Cardiff.

Auguste Renoir Book of 30 Postcards - BSB Publishing - The Hague - Holland

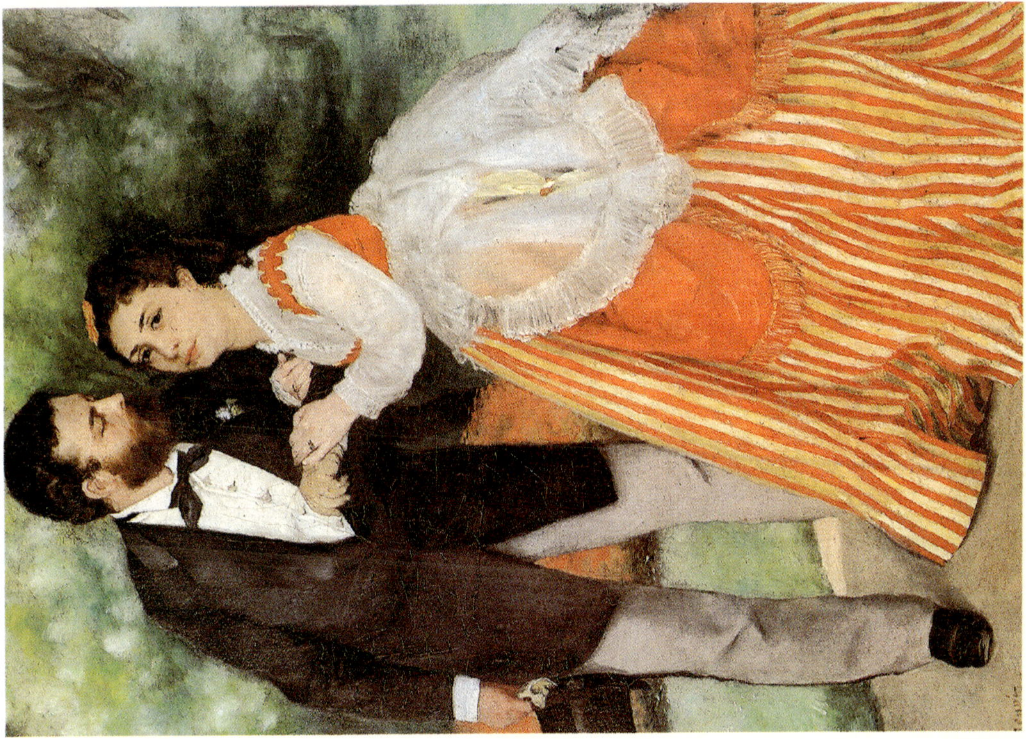

Auguste Renoir, *Portrait of Alfred and Marie Sisley,* 1868.
Wallraf-Richartz Museum, Cologne.

Auguste Renoir Book of 30 Postcards - BSB Publishing - The Hague - Holland

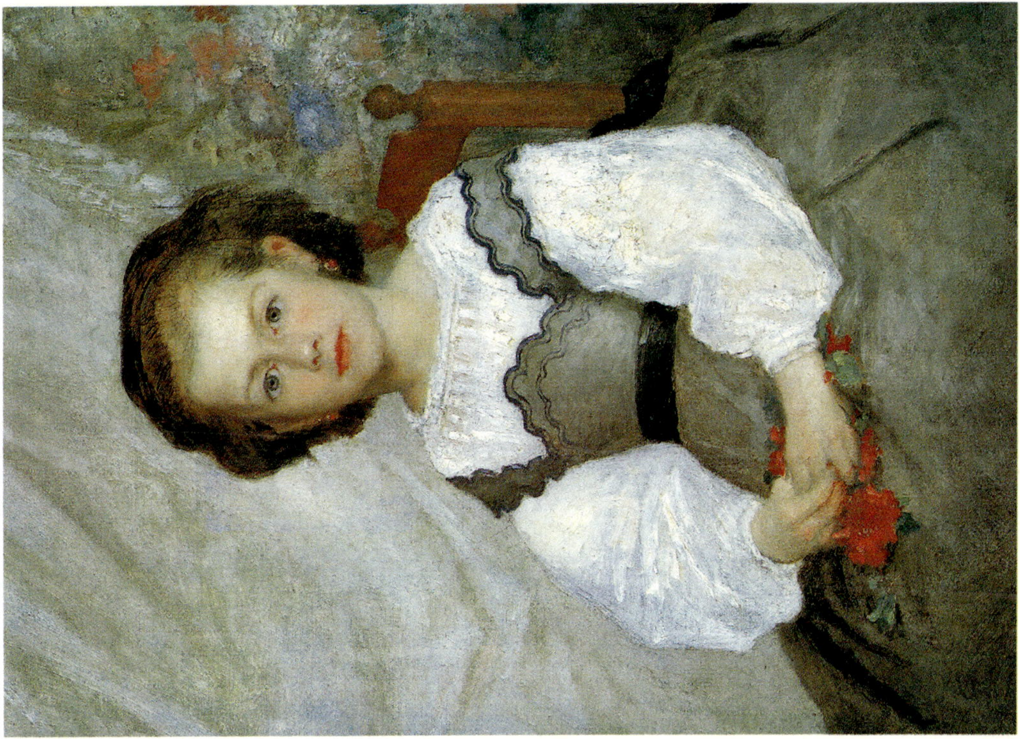

Auguste Renoir, *Romaine Lascaux,* 1864.
Museum of Art, Cleveland.

Auguste Renoir Book of 30 Postcards - BSB Publishing - The Hague - Holland

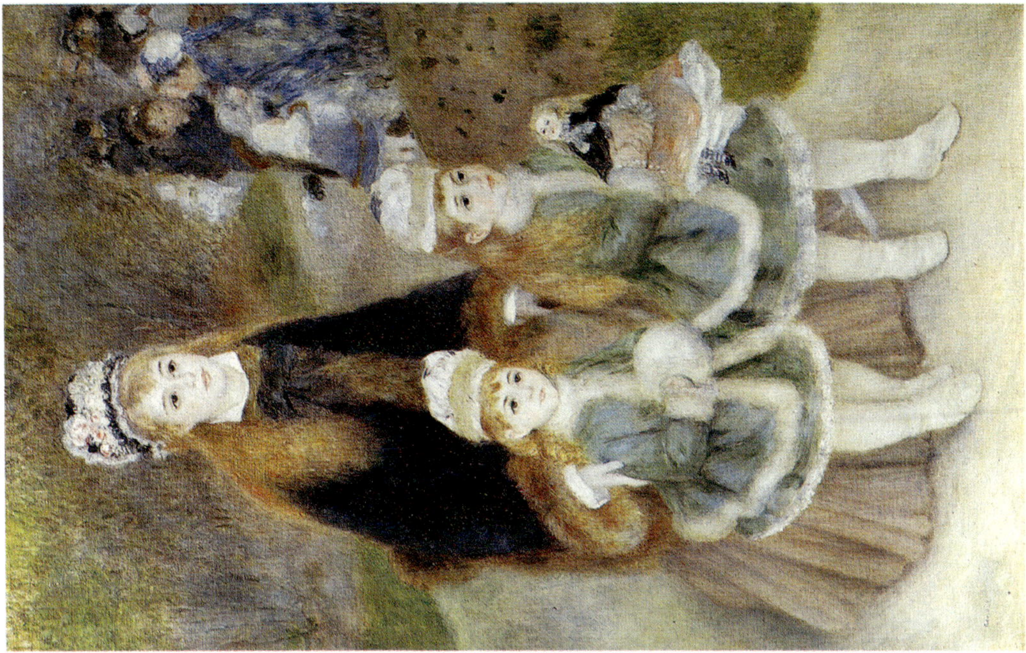

Auguste Renoir, *Mother Strolling with her Two Children*, 1875.
The Frick Collection, New York.

Auguste Renoir Book of 30 Postcards - BSB Publishing - The Hague - Holland

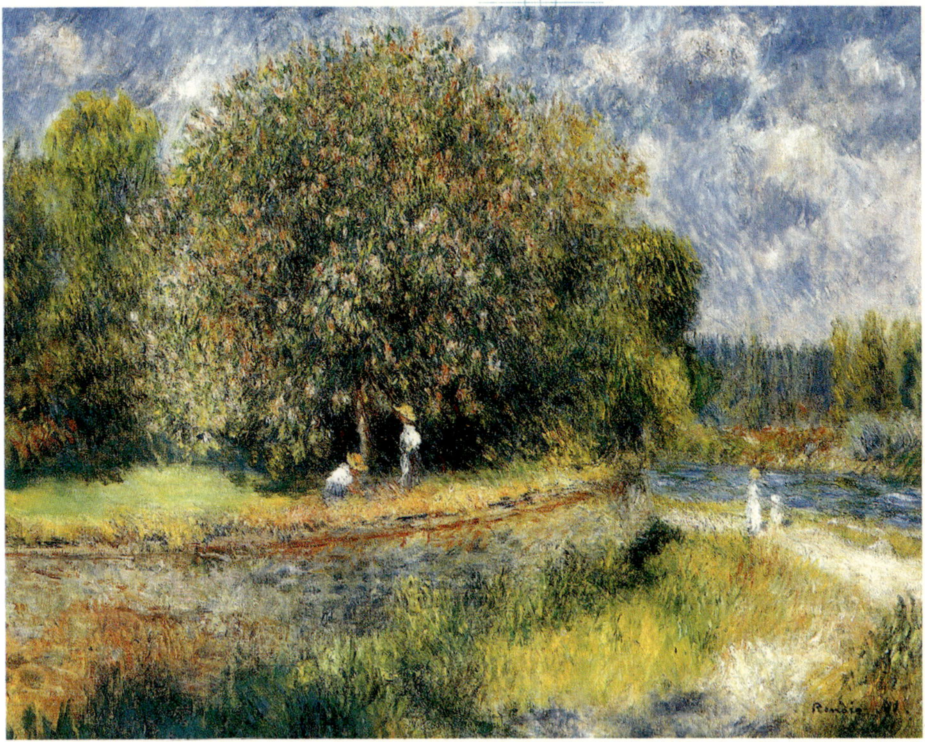

Auguste Renoir, *Blooming Chestnut Tree,* 1881.
Neue Nationalgalerie, Berlin.

Auguste Renoir Book of 30 Postcards - BSB Publishing - The Hague - Holland

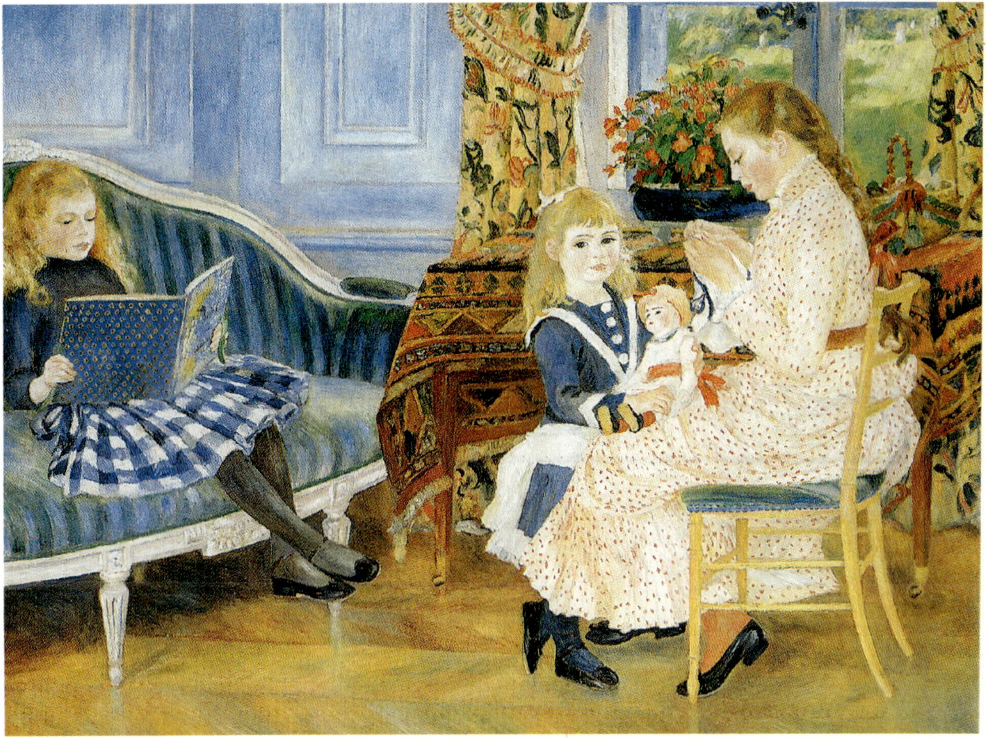

Auguste Renoir, *The Children's Afternoon at Waremont,* 1884.
Neue Nationalgalerie, Berlin.

Auguste Renoir Book of 30 Postcards - BSB Publishing - The Hague - Holland

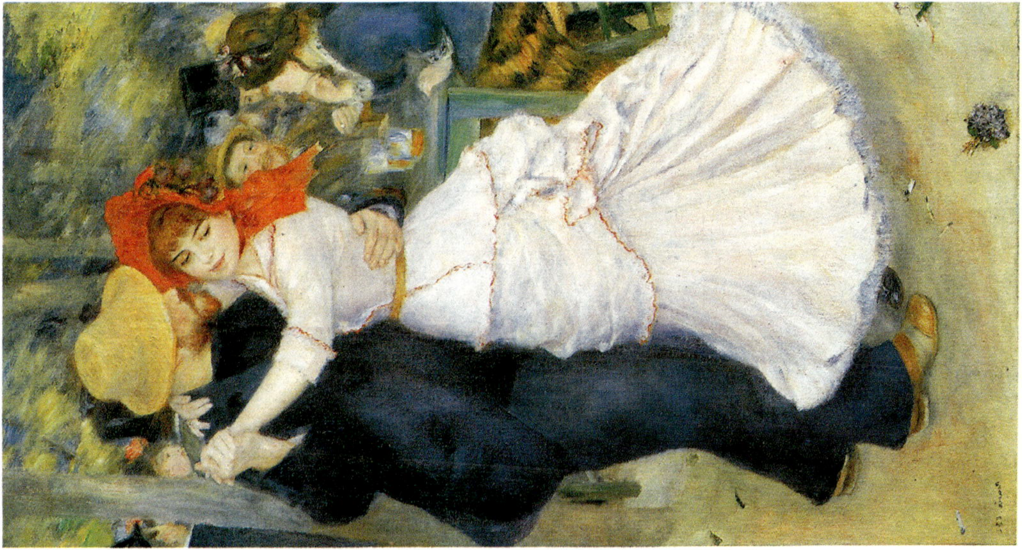

Auguste Renoir, *Dance at Bougival,* 1882-83.
Museum of Fine Arts, Boston.

Auguste Renoir Book of 30 Postcards - BSB Publishing - The Hague - Holland

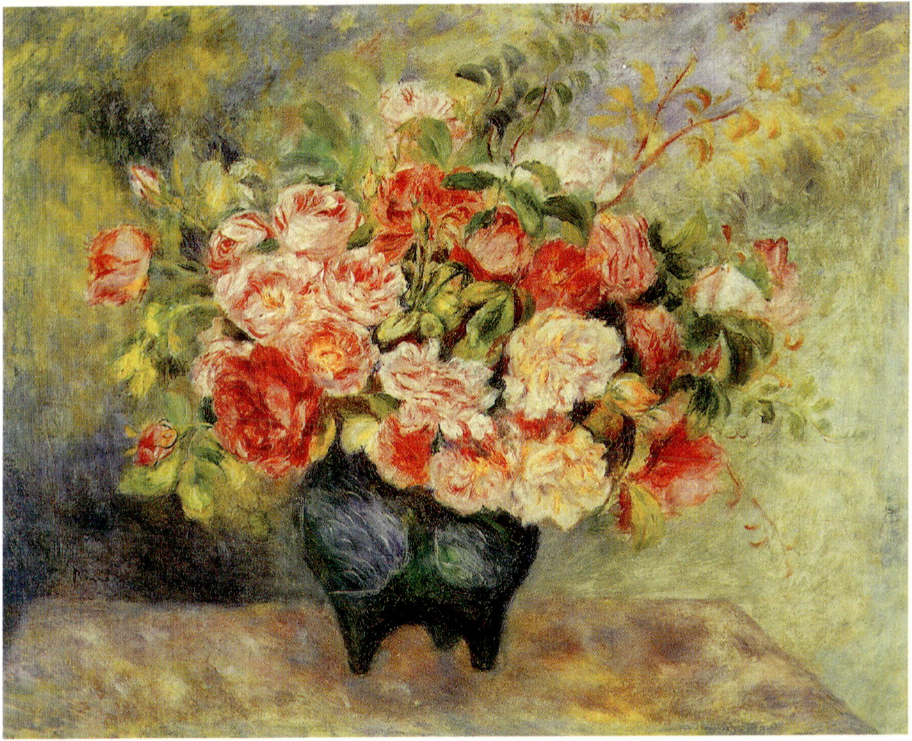

Auguste Renoir, *Bouquet of Flowers*, c. 1880-82.
Israel Museum, Jerusalem.

Auguste Renoir Book of 30 Postcards - BSB Publishing - The Hague - Holland

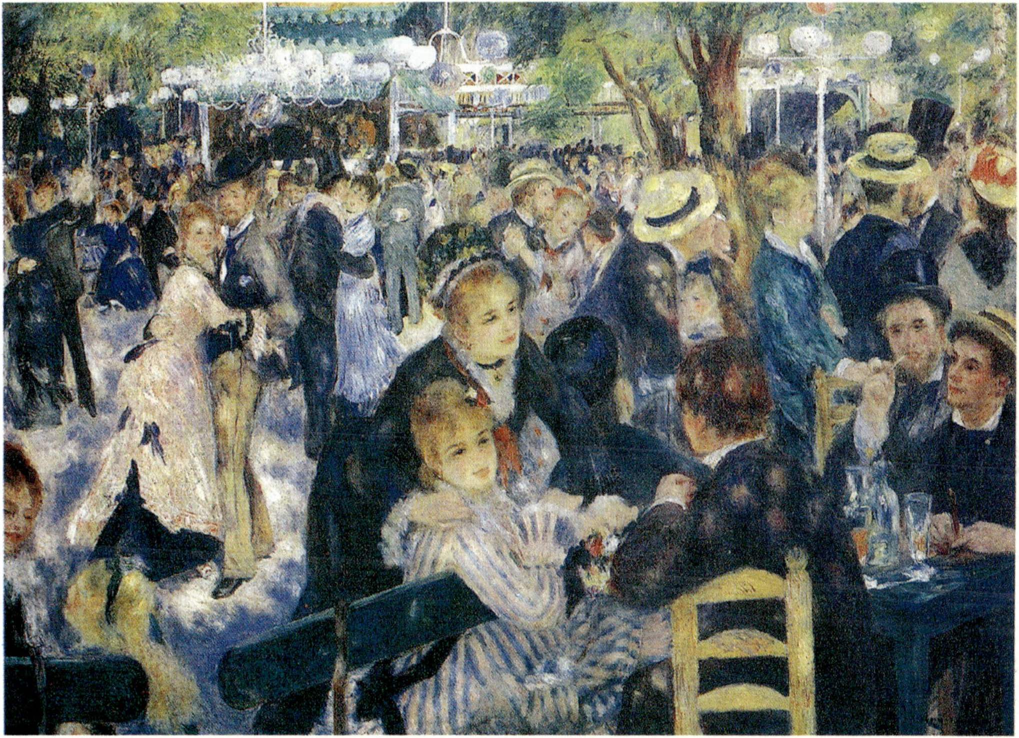

Auguste Renoir, *Ball at the Moulin de la Galette*, 1876.
Musée d'Orsay, Paris.

Auguste Renoir Book of 30 Postcards - BSB Publishing - The Hague - Holland

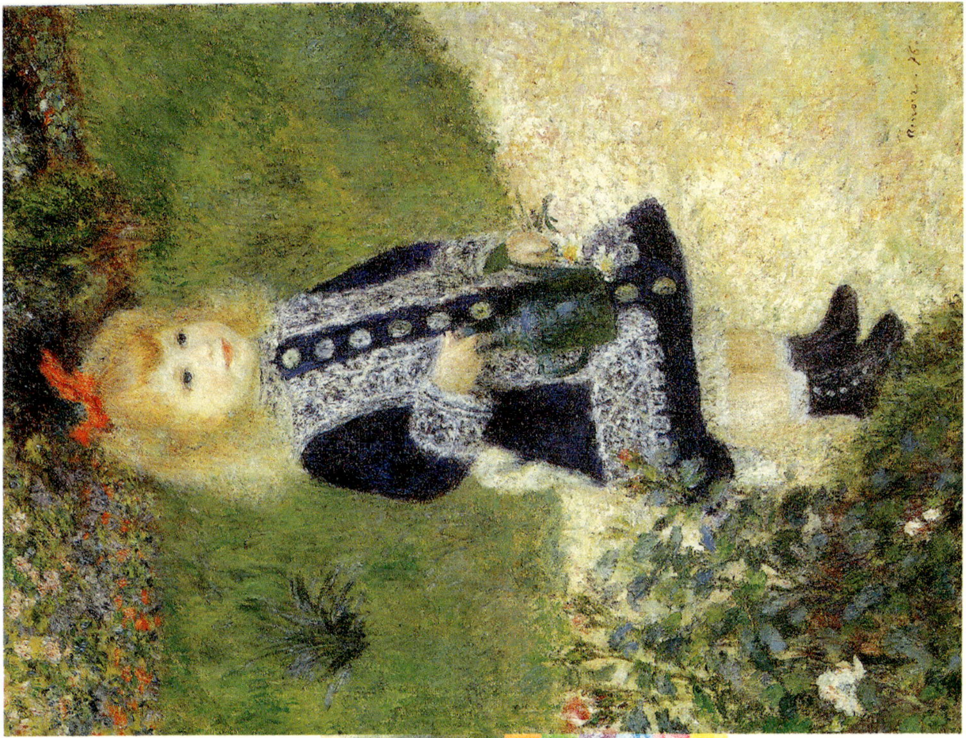

Auguste Renoir, *Girl with a Watering Can,* 1876.
National Gallery of Art, Washington D.C.

Auguste Renoir Book of 30 Postcards - BSB Publishing - The Hague - Holland